The Night of the censuS

by
Fran Key

Copyright (c) 2017 by Fran Key. All rights reserved.
First paperback edition printed 2017
Based on the poem 'T'was the night before Christmas'
attributed to Clement Clarke Moore.
A catalogue record for this book is available from the British Library.

ISBN: 978-0-9954770-1-8

Published by Lamb & Priestly

email: lambandpriestlypublishing@outlook.com

But when the fullness of the time was come,
GOD sent forth His SON,
made of a woman,
made under The Law,
Galatians 4:4

'Twas the night of the census,
when all through the shed
not a creature was stirring
they'd all gone to bed.

The stalls were all full
and their troughs filled with hay,
each animal had
a warm place where they lay.

And in the Inn too,
the people all slept,
while down in the stable
a vigil was kept;

A man and his wife,
who was due to give birth,
awaited their child
on a bed made of earth.

When all of a sudden
the peaceful night sky
was pierced by the sound
of a new baby's cry.

And at the Inn's windows
the faces came peeping,
with a newly born baby
few were still sleeping.

So out of the stable
and into the night,
"It's a Boy!" cried the father's voice
filled with delight;

Out in the courtyard
the guests could have glanced
at the proud new father
in joy as he danced.

And in the courtyard,
what did they see?
but a number of shepherds
come in sheepishly;

They bowed down in worship,
the babe they adored,
and went back into Town
loudly praising The Lord.

"It's just as the Angel
had said it would be!"
said the young shepherd boy,
his voice filled with glee.

"Let's tell everyone!"
his friends then enthused,
"We can't keep this quiet!
It's truly Good News!"

Now off in the east
as they gazed at the sky,
a new star was seen
by a group of Magi.

As they wondered together
just what this star meant,
they found that a new King
from Heaven was sent.

So off on a journey
they went forth to see
this Heavenly King
where 'ere He might be.

And off to the east
they started to ride.
No compass to lead them,
the star was their guide.

Now after some time
they came to the place,
and seeing the child
they fell on their face.

They offered Him gifts
which they laid at His feet,
gold, myrrh and incense,
it's perfume so sweet.

This baby was born
GOD's Salvation to bring,
He will soon come again
to be this worlds King.

He died for our sins
but raised up again
and ascended to Heaven
forever to reign.

And so, dear reader,
this story is true,
but now that you've heard it,
what will you do?

If you wish in your life
you could have a new start
open up and let JESUS
be born in your heart.

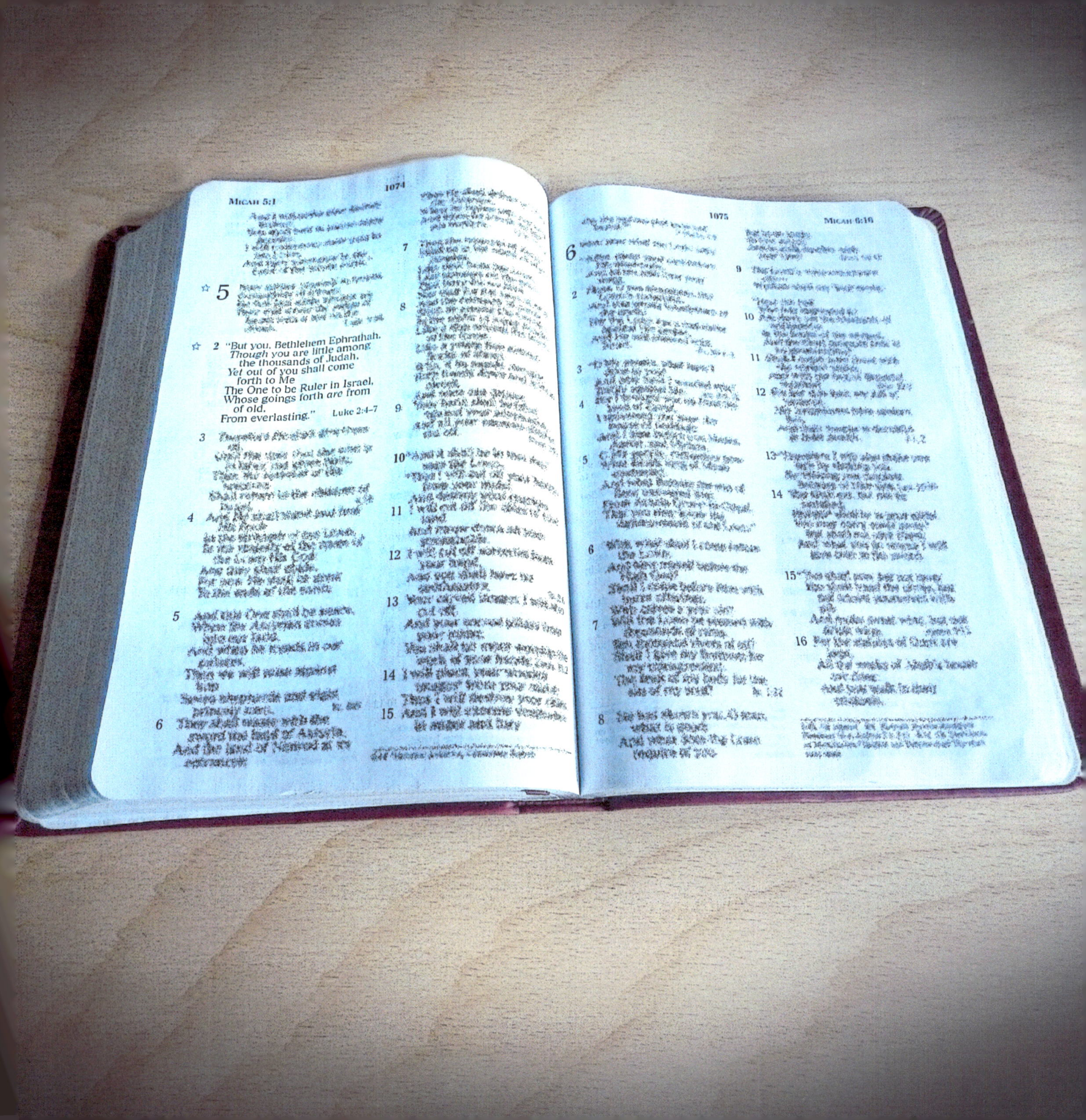
Micah 5:1
1074
5
2 "But you, Bethlehem Ephrathah,
Though you are little among
the thousands of Judah,
Yet out of you shall come
forth to Me
The One to be Ruler in Israel,
Whose goings forth are from
of old,
From everlasting." Luke 2:4–7
3
4
5
6
7
8
9
10
11
12
13
14
15
1075
Micah 6:16
6
2
3
4
5
6
7
8
9
10
11
12
13
14
15
16